Title: "Bitcoin Future"

This book, along with its contents encompassing text, illustrations, images, diagrams, and other creative elements, is the exclusive property of FAISAL JAMIL and is safeguarded by copyright law.

While efforts have been made to ensure accuracy and reliability, FAISAL JAMIL does not guarantee the completeness or suitability of the information. Readers are responsible for evaluating and using the content judiciously.

FAISAL JAMIL reserves the right to make changes, updates, or corrections to the book without prior notice. Inclusion of third-party materials or references does not imply

Warm regards,

FAISAL JAMIL

I Always Give's Free Copies Need Your Feedback And

Reviews Keeps In Touch!

http://www.amazon.com/author/faisal.jamil

Email: faisaljamilauthor@gmail.com

About the author

Certainly! Faisal Jamil is a multifaceted individual with a diverse set of skills and experiences. With a strong foundation in computer knowledge since childhood, he has developed a deep understanding of technology that informs his work as a content writer. Faisal also possesses digital skills, which further enhance his abilities in various digital platforms and technologies.

Beyond his professional endeavors, Faisal Jamil has also excelled in the martial arts, particularly Shotokan Karate, where he achieved the prestigious rank of first Dan black belt. This achievement speaks to his dedication, discipline, and commitment to personal growth and mastery.

In his professional life, Faisal Jamil has carved out a successful career in sales management within the Fast Moving Consumer Goods (FMCG) sector. His roles in various FMCG companies have honed his skills in strategic planning, team leadership, and business development. Faisal's ability to drive sales and achieve targets has been instrumental in his career progression, showcasing his talent for identifying opportunities and delivering results.

Faisal Jamil is also deeply interested in business investment strategies, planning, and execution. His understanding of these areas has been key to his success in the business world, allowing him to make informed decisions and implement effective strategies. His ability to navigate the complexities of investment planning and execution has set him apart as a strategic thinker and a valuable asset in any business endeavor.

Overall, Faisal Jamil is a dynamic individual who combines his passion for technology, martial arts, sales management, digital skills, and business investment strategies to achieve success in diverse fields. His journey is a testament to his versatility, resilience, and continuous pursuit of excellence.

Yours Sincerely

FAISAL JAMIL

I Always Give's Free Copies Need Your Feedback And

Reviews Keeps In Touch!

https://www.amazon.com/author/faisal.jamil

Email: faisaljamilauthor@gmail.com

BITCOIN FUTURE

Table of Content

INTRODUCTION

To Bitcoin Future

In the ever-evolving landscape of global finance, few innovations have sparked as much intrigue, debate, and transformation as Bitcoin. Born from the mind of the enigmatic Satoshi Nakamoto, Bitcoin emerged in 2009 as a radical departure from traditional financial systems. Its promise of decentralization, transparency, and financial sovereignty challenged the very foundations of how we perceive and handle money.

Bitcoin Future embarks on a journey through the transformative evolution of this digital currency, tracing its origins, trials, and triumphs. This book delves into the complexities and nuances that have defined Bitcoin's path, offering a comprehensive exploration of its impact on financial markets, technological advancements, and societal structures.

The journey begins with the creation of the Genesis Block, the cornerstone of Bitcoin's blockchain, and the early days of adoption marked by excitement and skepticism. From there, we navigate through the turbulent boom and bust cycles, including the infamous Mt. Gox collapse and the subsequent resilience that has characterized Bitcoin's growth.

As Bitcoin started to garner mainstream acceptance, institutional investors and regulatory bodies began to take notice, leading to significant developments in financial products and legal frameworks. This acceptance was further bolstered by technological advancements, which addressed scalability and usability issues, paving the way for broader adoption and integration into various sectors.

Bitcoin Future also examines the profound global impact of Bitcoin. It has offered financial inclusion to those in unstable economies, influenced central banks to explore digital currencies, and provided a tool for freedom and privacy in oppressive regimes. These aspects highlight Bitcoin's role not just as a financial asset but as a catalyst for economic and sociopolitical change.

Looking ahead, we explore Bitcoin's potential future horizons. As it solidifies its position as "digital gold," we consider its growing role in investment portfolios and as a global reserve asset. We also delve into the exciting possibilities of Bitcoin's integration with emerging technologies like artificial intelligence and the Internet of Things, and its influence on societal values such as decentralization, transparency, and individual sovereignty.

Bitcoin Future is not just a chronicle of a digital currency but a narrative of innovation, disruption, and the relentless pursuit of a new financial paradigm. Whether you are a seasoned investor, a technology enthusiast, or someone curious about the future of money, this book offers insights into how Bitcoin is reshaping our world and what lies ahead in this revolutionary journey.

Chapter 1

The Dawn of Digital Currency

Branch 1: Genesis Block

In the early 2000s, the idea of a digital currency was often dismissed as a futuristic fantasy, far removed from reality. However, the landscape of finance was about to change dramatically. On January 3, 2009, a monumental event occurred that would pave the way for a new era in financial technology: the creation of Bitcoin's Genesis Block by the enigmatic figure known as Satoshi Nakamoto.

The Genesis Block, or Block 0, was the first block of the Bitcoin blockchain. It was more than just a technical achievement; it was a declaration of a new paradigm. Embedded within the code of this block was a cryptic message: "The Times 03/Jan/2009 Chancellor on brink of second bailout for banks." This phrase, referencing a headline from The Times newspaper, was a pointed commentary on the existing financial system's fragility and the repeated bailouts of major banks by governments.

Satoshi Nakamoto's choice to embed this message was not merely symbolic; it was a clear articulation of Bitcoin's purpose. Bitcoin was conceived as a decentralized financial system, free from the control of central banks and government interference. It was designed to be a peer-to-peer digital currency that empowered individuals, allowing them to transact directly without relying on traditional financial institutions. The Genesis Block was not just the birth of Bitcoin but the beginning of a financial revolution aimed at creating a more transparent, secure, and autonomous economic system.

The mystery surrounding Nakamoto's identity only added to the intrigue of Bitcoin. Speculations ranged from it being a single genius programmer to a collective of developers. Despite the anonymity, Nakamoto's creation rapidly garnered attention from a small, yet passionate group of cryptographers and libertarians who saw the potential in this novel technology.

Branch 2: Early Adoption and Skepticism

The initial reception of Bitcoin was marked by a blend of enthusiasm and doubt. Early adopters, primarily comprising tech enthusiasts, cryptographers, and libertarians, were captivated by the idea of a decentralized currency that could operate outside the purview of governments and financial institutions. These pioneers were drawn to Bitcoin's promise of financial sovereignty, privacy, and the elimination of middlemen in transactions.

One of the first significant uses of Bitcoin was by early adopters to experiment with its functionality, trade amongst themselves, and purchase goods and services within a growing but niche ecosystem. Websites like BitcoinTalk and various online forums became hubs for discussions, technical development, and community building.

However, Bitcoin also faced considerable skepticism. Mainstream economists and financial experts were quick to label it as a speculative bubble, predicting its imminent collapse. Government officials expressed concerns about its potential use for illegal activities due to the pseudonymous nature of transactions. Media outlets often portrayed Bitcoin as a curious, albeit risky, experiment.

Despite the mixed reactions, the Bitcoin community remained undeterred. Developers continuously worked on improving the software, addressing technical challenges, and enhancing security. Entrepreneurs began to establish Bitcoin exchanges, wallets, and other infrastructure to support the growing ecosystem. As more people learned about Bitcoin and its underlying blockchain technology, the network's user base expanded, and Bitcoin started to gain traction as a legitimate financial asset.

Branch 3: The Silk Road Era

One of the pivotal moments in Bitcoin's early history was its association with the Silk Road, an online marketplace that operated on the dark web. Founded in 2011 by Ross Ulbricht, the Silk Road used Bitcoin as its primary currency due to its perceived anonymity, which made it an ideal medium for transactions on the black market.

The Silk Road quickly gained notoriety for enabling the sale of illegal goods, including drugs and counterfeit items. While this association painted Bitcoin in a negative light, it also showcased its practical applications. Bitcoin's use on the Silk Road demonstrated its potential for secure and anonymous transactions, drawing attention to its unique properties and igniting debates about digital privacy and financial freedom.

The success of the Silk Road and the subsequent media coverage significantly increased public awareness of Bitcoin. However, it also attracted the scrutiny of law enforcement agencies. In 2013, the FBI shut down the Silk Road and arrested Ross Ulbricht, seizing millions of dollars' worth of Bitcoin in the process. This event marked a turning point for Bitcoin, highlighting the urgent need for legal and regulatory frameworks to address the challenges posed by digital currencies.

The Silk Road era underscored the dual-edged nature of Bitcoin. On one hand, it was a groundbreaking technology with the potential to revolutionize finance; on the other, it was a tool that could be misused for illicit activities. The subsequent regulatory actions and legal developments aimed to strike a balance between fostering innovation and ensuring compliance with existing laws.

As Bitcoin emerged from the shadow of the Silk Road, it began to forge a more legitimate path. The focus shifted towards its potential for mainstream adoption, technological innovation, and the broader implications for the global financial system. The dawn of digital currency was just beginning, setting the stage for the transformative journey that lay ahead.

Chapter 2

Bitcoin Boom and Bust

Branch 1: The 2013 Bull Run

In 2013, Bitcoin captured the world's attention with its first significant bull run. The price of a single Bitcoin skyrocketed from under $100 in January to over $1,000 by November. This dramatic increase in value was driven by several factors, including increasing media coverage, growing adoption by merchants and consumers, and a surge in speculative investment.

The media frenzy played a crucial role in Bitcoin's meteoric rise. News outlets around the globe began to cover Bitcoin extensively, highlighting stories of early adopters who had made fortunes and exploring the potential of blockchain technology. This coverage fueled public interest and curiosity, attracting a new wave of investors eager to capitalize on the rising prices.

Merchants and businesses also began to accept Bitcoin as a payment method, further legitimizing its use as a currency. Major companies like Overstock.com announced they would accept Bitcoin, signaling a shift towards broader acceptance. This growing adoption contributed to the increasing demand for Bitcoin, driving prices even higher.

However, the rapid rise in Bitcoin's value also attracted speculative investors looking for quick profits. The influx of speculative money led to a volatile market, with prices swinging wildly. By December 2013, Bitcoin had reached its peak, trading at over $1,150 on some exchanges. Yet, this high was short-lived.

As quickly as Bitcoin's value had surged, it began to decline. By the end of December, prices had fallen by more than

50%, leading to widespread criticism and skepticism. Many financial analysts and media commentators declared Bitcoin a speculative bubble that had burst, predicting its demise. Despite these proclamations, the underlying technology and the community supporting Bitcoin continued to evolve and strengthen.

Branch 2: Mt. Gox Collapse

The fragility of the Bitcoin ecosystem was starkly highlighted by the collapse of Mt. Gox in 2014. Mt. Gox, based in Tokyo, was the largest Bitcoin exchange in the world, handling over 70% of all Bitcoin transactions at its peak. Its failure marked a significant crisis for the nascent cryptocurrency industry.

The collapse began with the exchange suspending withdrawals in February 2014, citing technical issues. Soon after, it was revealed that Mt. Gox had been the victim of a massive hack, resulting in the loss of approximately 850,000 Bitcoins, worth about $450 million at the time. The hack, combined with alleged mismanagement and financial irregularities, led to the exchange declaring bankruptcy.

The Mt. Gox debacle had far-reaching implications. It shattered investor confidence, leading to a sharp decline in Bitcoin's price and sparking fears about the security of cryptocurrency exchanges. Many investors lost significant amounts of money, leading to lawsuits and regulatory scrutiny.

The collapse underscored the urgent need for better security measures and regulatory oversight in the cryptocurrency industry. It highlighted the risks associated with centralized exchanges and the importance of robust security practices. In the aftermath, the Bitcoin community and industry stakeholders began to push for more secure and transparent practices, laying the groundwork for future improvements.

Branch 3: Resilience and Recovery

Despite the significant setbacks of 2013's price crash and the Mt. Gox collapse, Bitcoin demonstrated remarkable resilience. The community of developers, entrepreneurs, and enthusiasts continued to work on improving the technology and infrastructure surrounding Bitcoin, leading to a period of recovery and growth.

One of the key areas of focus was security. The Mt. Gox incident prompted a re-evaluation of security practices within the industry. New exchanges and platforms emerged, incorporating advanced security measures such as multi-signature wallets, cold storage solutions, and regular audits. These improvements helped to restore confidence in the security of Bitcoin transactions and exchanges.

Scalability was another critical issue that developers addressed. The Bitcoin network faced challenges in handling an increasing number of transactions, leading to higher fees and slower processing times. Innovations like the Lightning Network were developed to address these issues by enabling faster and cheaper transactions off the main blockchain. These technological advancements improved the usability and efficiency of Bitcoin, making it more accessible to a broader audience.

Additionally, regulatory developments played a significant role in the recovery process. Governments and regulatory bodies began to develop frameworks to address the unique challenges posed by cryptocurrencies. While some countries imposed strict regulations, others adopted a more favorable stance, recognizing the potential of blockchain technology. This evolving regulatory landscape provided a clearer path for the legitimate use and development of Bitcoin.

The Bitcoin community's commitment to decentralization and transparency remained a driving force behind its resilience. Open-source development and decentralized governance ensured that no single entity could control the network, fostering innovation and trust. This ethos helped to attract new developers and entrepreneurs, leading to a vibrant ecosystem of applications and services built on top of Bitcoin.

As Bitcoin emerged from the tumultuous period of boom and bust, it was stronger and more robust. The lessons learned from the early challenges paved the way for future growth and adoption. Bitcoin's journey through the boom and bust cycle highlighted its potential as a revolutionary technology and set the stage for its continued evolution as a digital currency and financial asset.

Chapter 3

Mainstream Acceptance

Branch 1: Institutional Investment

By the late 2010s, the financial landscape had begun to shift dramatically in favor of Bitcoin. What was once considered a fringe asset, favored primarily by tech enthusiasts and libertarians, started to gain serious attention from institutional investors. This marked a pivotal moment in Bitcoin's journey toward mainstream acceptance.

Institutional investors, including major financial institutions, hedge funds, and publicly traded companies, began to recognize Bitcoin's potential as a store of value and a hedge against inflation. The economic environment of the late 2010s, characterized by low interest rates and expansive monetary policies, heightened concerns about the devaluation of traditional currencies. Bitcoin, with its fixed supply of 21 million coins, presented a compelling alternative.

One of the most significant endorsements came from large publicly traded companies. In 2020, MicroStrategy, a business intelligence firm, announced it had invested over $1 billion in Bitcoin, citing it as a superior store of value compared to cash. This move was followed by other notable companies, such as Tesla, which added Bitcoin to its balance sheet. These high-profile investments brought unprecedented legitimacy to Bitcoin and sparked a wave of interest from other corporations and institutional investors.

The involvement of institutional investors brought increased stability to the cryptocurrency market. Unlike retail investors, institutions often have a longer-term investment horizon and employ sophisticated risk management strategies. Their participation also led to the development of new financial products, such as Bitcoin futures and exchange-traded funds (ETFs), which provided more avenues for investment and greater market liquidity.

Moreover, the entry of institutional money spurred the creation of more robust and compliant infrastructure. Custodial services, which offer secure storage solutions for large amounts of Bitcoin, became a critical component of the ecosystem. Companies like Fidelity Digital Assets and Coinbase Custody emerged as trusted custodians, addressing security concerns and making it easier for institutional investors to hold Bitcoin.

Branch 2: Regulatory Developments

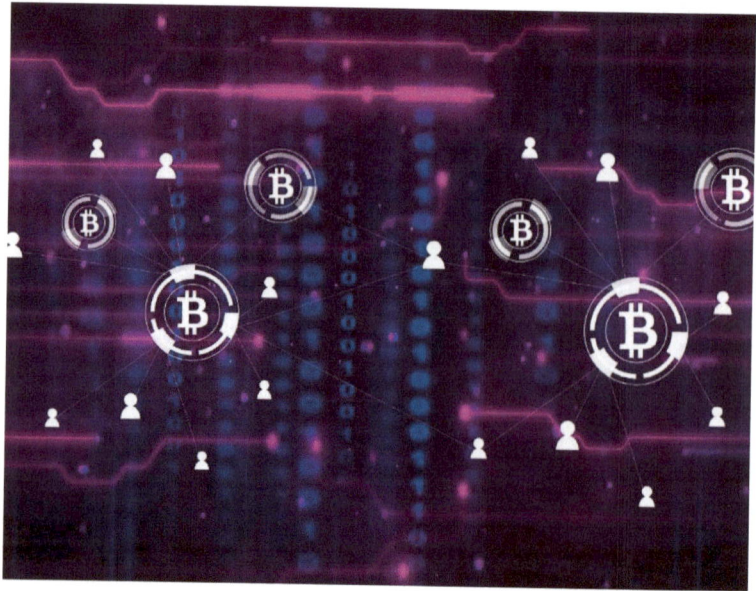

As Bitcoin began to gain traction among institutional investors and the broader public, governments and regulatory bodies worldwide started to take a closer look at cryptocurrencies. The need for a regulatory framework became increasingly evident to balance consumer protection, prevent illicit activities, and foster innovation.

In the United States, the Securities and Exchange Commission (SEC) and the Commodity Futures Trading Commission (CFTC) played crucial roles in shaping the regulatory landscape. The SEC focused on determining whether various cryptocurrency offerings qualified as securities, while the CFTC regulated Bitcoin as a commodity. This distinction was essential in providing clarity and legal guidance for businesses and investors.

One of the landmark developments was the approval of Bitcoin futures trading by the CFTC. In December 2017, the Chicago Mercantile Exchange (CME) and the Chicago Board Options Exchange (CBOE) launched Bitcoin futures contracts, allowing investors to speculate on the future price of Bitcoin. This move was seen as a significant step towards integrating Bitcoin into the mainstream financial system.

In Europe, regulatory approaches varied across countries. The European Union took steps to develop a unified regulatory framework through initiatives like the Markets in Crypto-Assets (MiCA) regulation. MiCA aimed to create a comprehensive set of rules for digital assets, ensuring investor protection and market integrity while fostering innovation.

In contrast, some countries took a more restrictive approach. China, for instance, imposed a series of crackdowns on cryptocurrency trading and mining, citing concerns over financial stability and illicit activities. These actions highlighted the divergent regulatory approaches and the global complexity of cryptocurrency regulation.

Despite varying regulatory stances, the overall trend was towards greater clarity and oversight. Regulatory developments provided a foundation for legitimate businesses to operate and reassured investors about the legal status of their investments. This evolving regulatory landscape played a crucial role in shaping the future of Bitcoin and the broader cryptocurrency market.

Branch 3: Technological Advancements

As Bitcoin continued to gain mainstream acceptance, technological advancements became imperative to address scalability, transaction speed, and privacy concerns. These enhancements were crucial in making Bitcoin more practical for everyday use and ensuring its sustainability.

One of the significant technological developments was the implementation of the Lightning Network. The Lightning Network is a second-layer solution designed to enable faster and cheaper transactions by conducting transactions off-chain. This innovation addressed Bitcoin's scalability issues, allowing for a higher volume of transactions without congesting the main blockchain. The Lightning Network made Bitcoin more viable for small, everyday transactions, such as buying a cup of coffee, and opened up new use cases.

Another important upgrade was Segregated Witness (SegWit), which was activated in 2017. SegWit improved the efficiency of Bitcoin transactions by separating the transaction signatures from the transaction data. This change effectively increased the block size limit, allowing more transactions to be processed in each block. SegWit also laid the groundwork for further innovations, such as the Lightning Network.

In 2021, the Taproot upgrade was introduced, bringing enhanced privacy and smart contract functionality to Bitcoin. Taproot improved privacy by making all transactions look the same on the blockchain, whether they were simple payments or complex smart contracts. This upgrade also made it possible to create more sophisticated and flexible smart contracts, expanding Bitcoin's functionality beyond simple transactions.

These technological advancements addressed many of the criticisms regarding Bitcoin's usability and environmental impact. By improving scalability and transaction efficiency, these upgrades reduced the carbon footprint associated with Bitcoin mining and transactions. They also made Bitcoin more practical for a broader range of applications, paving the way for wider adoption.

The combination of institutional investment, regulatory developments, and technological advancements marked a new era of mainstream acceptance for Bitcoin. What began as a fringe technology had transformed into a legitimate financial asset, with a robust infrastructure and a clear regulatory framework. Bitcoin's journey from its early days to mainstream acceptance highlighted its potential to revolutionize the financial system and set the stage for its continued evolution and integration into the global economy.

Chapter 4

The Global Impact

Branch 1: Financial Inclusion

Bitcoin's decentralized nature offered a revolutionary solution for financial inclusion, particularly in regions with unstable economies and limited access to traditional banking services. For billions of people around the world, traditional banking infrastructure was either inaccessible or unreliable, creating significant barriers to economic participation. Bitcoin and other cryptocurrencies presented a way to overcome these barriers.

In many developing countries, hyperinflation and political instability eroded trust in national currencies and financial institutions. Bitcoin, with its fixed supply and decentralized control, provided an alternative store of value that was not subject to the whims of government policies or economic mismanagement. Individuals in countries like Venezuela and Zimbabwe, where local currencies had become virtually worthless, began turning to Bitcoin to preserve their wealth.

Bitcoin's digital and borderless nature also made it accessible to anyone with an internet connection. This accessibility was crucial in regions where physical banking infrastructure was lacking. Mobile phone penetration was high even in many low-income countries, allowing people to use their devices to access Bitcoin wallets and conduct transactions. This shift empowered individuals by giving them direct control over their finances without needing a bank account.

Small businesses in these regions also benefited from the ability to conduct cross-border transactions without the need for costly and slow intermediaries. Bitcoin's low transaction fees and faster settlement times compared to traditional banking systems made it an attractive option for remittances and international trade. This ease of use and cost-effectiveness opened up new economic opportunities and facilitated greater participation in the global economy.

Moreover, Bitcoin's decentralized nature meant that it could operate in environments where trust in central authorities was low. People could conduct transactions peer-to-peer, bypassing potentially corrupt or inefficient banking systems. This financial empowerment was particularly significant for marginalized groups who had historically been excluded from formal financial systems.

Branch 2: Economic Shifts

As Bitcoin gained traction, its influence on global economic dynamics became increasingly evident. Central banks and governments around the world started to take notice, leading to a new era of financial innovation and competition. The rise of Bitcoin and other cryptocurrencies prompted central banks to explore the development of their own digital currencies, known as Central Bank Digital Currencies (CBDCs).

CBDCs aimed to modernize financial systems and offer a state-controlled alternative to decentralized cryptocurrencies. Countries like China, Sweden, and the Bahamas took the lead in developing and testing CBDCs, with others following suit. These digital currencies promised to enhance the efficiency of payment systems, reduce transaction costs, and increase financial inclusion.

The introduction of CBDCs also represented a shift in how money was created, managed, and transferred. Traditional banking systems relied on intermediaries like commercial banks to facilitate transactions. In contrast, CBDCs could enable direct peer-to-peer transactions, reducing the need for intermediaries and potentially lowering the cost of financial services.

Bitcoin's impact extended beyond the realm of digital currencies. It spurred innovation in financial technology (fintech), leading to the development of new financial products and services. Decentralized finance (DeFi) platforms, built on blockchain technology, offered alternatives to traditional banking services such as lending, borrowing, and trading. These platforms operated without central authorities, relying instead on smart contracts to execute transactions automatically.

The competition between decentralized cryptocurrencies, CBDCs, and traditional financial systems reshaped the global financial landscape. Central banks and financial institutions had to adapt to the changing environment, embracing digital transformation to stay relevant. This period of rapid innovation and competition led to a more dynamic and inclusive global financial system.

Branch 3: Sociopolitical Implications

Bitcoin's rise also had profound sociopolitical implications, influencing how people interacted with financial systems and challenging existing power structures. Its decentralized and censorship-resistant nature made it a powerful tool for individuals living under oppressive regimes or facing political instability.

In countries with authoritarian governments, Bitcoin offered a means of financial freedom and privacy.

Dissidents and activists could use Bitcoin to fund their activities without fear of government surveillance or asset seizure. For example, in Belarus during the 2020 protests against President Alexander Lukashenko, Bitcoin provided a way for protesters to receive donations and support from international communities without interference from the state.

Bitcoin's ability to operate independently of central authorities also posed challenges for law enforcement and national security. Its pseudonymous nature made it attractive for illicit activities such as money laundering, drug trafficking, and ransomware attacks. Governments and regulatory bodies struggled to find a balance between preventing illegal activities and preserving the freedoms that Bitcoin offered.

The debate over Bitcoin's regulation became a central issue in its ongoing evolution. On one side, proponents argued that Bitcoin's decentralized nature was essential for financial freedom and innovation. They emphasized the importance of privacy and the right to conduct transactions without government interference. On the other side, critics pointed to the risks of unregulated financial systems and the potential for abuse by criminals.

The sociopolitical impact of Bitcoin extended beyond financial transactions. It inspired a broader movement towards decentralization and self-sovereignty. Concepts such as decentralized governance, where communities make decisions collectively without a central authority, gained traction. This movement influenced other areas, including data privacy, digital identity, and online communication.

As Bitcoin continued to evolve, it played a significant role in shaping the future of global finance and governance. Its impact on financial inclusion, economic dynamics, and sociopolitical structures highlighted its transformative potential and set the stage for ongoing debates about the role of decentralized technologies in society.

Chapter 5

Future Horizons

Branch 1: Bitcoin as Digital Gold

In the not-so-distant future, Bitcoin solidifies its status as "digital gold," establishing itself as a premier store of value and a reliable hedge against economic uncertainty. As global economic landscapes evolve, Bitcoin's finite supply and increasing demand make it a cornerstone asset in diversified investment portfolios worldwide.

Institutional investors and individual savers alike turn to Bitcoin to safeguard their wealth against inflation, currency devaluation, and geopolitical instability. Its role as a "safe haven" asset grows, paralleling the historical function of gold. Bitcoin's decentralized nature and transparent supply mechanics provide a level of security and predictability that fiat currencies, subject to the whims of central banks, cannot match.

As more nations recognize Bitcoin's value, its influence on monetary policy and global financial stability becomes evident. Central banks and financial institutions incorporate Bitcoin into their reserves, enhancing their ability to hedge against market fluctuations. This adoption further legitimizes Bitcoin, driving its integration into mainstream financial systems.

The concept of a global reserve asset takes on new meaning with Bitcoin at its core. Countries experiencing economic turmoil increasingly use Bitcoin to stabilize their financial systems. This shift prompts a rethinking of traditional financial models and encourages international cooperation in establishing new frameworks for digital assets.

Bitcoin's maturation into digital gold also impacts retail investors. With greater access to Bitcoin through regulated exchanges and financial products, individuals around the world can participate in the global financial system more equitably. This democratization of wealth-building tools fosters greater financial inclusion and resilience.

Branch 2: Technological Integration

The integration of Bitcoin with emerging technologies such as artificial intelligence (AI), the Internet of Things (IoT), and blockchain-based applications opens up a new frontier of possibilities. These synergies drive innovation and create novel solutions across various sectors.

Smart contracts, built on Bitcoin's secure and decentralized network, revolutionize how agreements are made and executed. These self-executing contracts reduce the need for intermediaries, cutting costs and increasing efficiency in industries ranging from real estate to supply chain management. Bitcoin's robustness ensures the integrity and reliability of these contracts, making them a preferred choice for complex and high-value transactions.

Decentralized finance (DeFi) platforms leverage Bitcoin to offer a range of financial services, including lending, borrowing, and trading, without the need for traditional banks. Bitcoin's security and network effects provide a solid foundation for these platforms, fostering trust and attracting users. This democratization of financial services empowers individuals and small businesses, particularly in underserved regions.

Decentralized autonomous organizations (DAOs) use Bitcoin to manage assets and operations transparently and efficiently. These organizations operate without central leadership, relying on code to enforce rules and distribute resources. Bitcoin's integration with DAOs enables new forms of governance and collaboration, driving innovation in organizational structures and business models.

In the realm of IoT, Bitcoin facilitates secure machine-to-machine transactions. Devices connected to the internet can use Bitcoin to autonomously execute transactions, enabling seamless and efficient interactions. This capability is particularly valuable in sectors such as logistics, where automated payments can streamline operations and reduce costs.

AI technologies enhance Bitcoin's utility by providing advanced analytics and predictive capabilities. AI algorithms analyze blockchain data to detect patterns and trends, offering insights that drive smarter investment strategies and fraud prevention measures. The combination of AI and Bitcoin creates a powerful tool for navigating the complexities of the digital economy.

Branch 3: Societal Transformation

Bitcoin's influence extends far beyond the financial realm, promoting the principles of decentralization, transparency, and individual sovereignty. These values drive a broader societal transformation, reshaping governance, data privacy, and digital identity.

The decentralization ethos championed by Bitcoin inspires new models of governance that prioritize citizen participation and transparency. Local and national governments experiment with blockchain-based voting systems, ensuring secure and tamper-proof elections. These systems enhance trust in democratic processes and empower citizens to have a direct say in policy decisions.

Data privacy emerges as a critical issue in the digital age, and Bitcoin's principles play a pivotal role in addressing it. Decentralized technologies offer alternatives to centralized data storage, reducing the risk of breaches and misuse. Individuals gain greater control over their personal information, deciding how and with whom it is shared. This shift promotes a more equitable digital environment where privacy is a fundamental right.

Digital identity systems built on blockchain technology offer secure and portable identities that individuals can use across various services. These systems reduce the need for redundant data collection and streamline access to essential services, from banking to healthcare. Bitcoin's underlying technology ensures the security and integrity of these identities, fostering trust and efficiency.

Bitcoin's impact on society also fosters a more open and equitable global economy. By enabling peer-to-peer transactions and reducing reliance on intermediaries, Bitcoin lowers barriers to economic participation. Individuals in developing countries, previously excluded from global markets, can now engage in international trade and commerce, driving economic growth and development.

As Bitcoin continues to evolve, it shapes the future of the internet and the global economy. Its principles influence the development of new technologies and systems, creating a more decentralized, transparent, and inclusive world. Bitcoin's legacy is not just as a digital currency but as a catalyst for profound societal change, leaving an indelible mark on human history.